Hello, My name is Max and I Have Autism

An Insight into the Autistic Mind
By Max Miller.

Edited by Joe Bonadonna.

Photography by Rebecca Miller

AuthorHouse™
1663 Liberty Drive
Bloomington, IN 47403
www.authorhouse.com
Phone: 833-262-8899

Because of the dynamic nature of the Internet, any web addresses or links contained in this book may have changed
since publication and may no longer be valid. The views expressed in this work are solely those of the author and do not
necessarily reflect the views of the publisher, and the publisher hereby disclaims any responsibility for them.

Any people depicted in stock imagery provided by Getty Images are models,
and such images are being used for illustrative purposes only.
Certain stock imagery © Getty Images.

This book is printed on acid-free paper.

ISBN: 978-1-4969-2298-4 (sc)
ISBN: 978-1-6655-3659-2 (hc)
ISBN: 978-1-4969-2299-1 (e)

Print information available on the last page.

Published by AuthorHouse 09/14/2021

authorHOUSE®

To all of us who are on the spectrum--together, we spark--Max Miller.

FORWARD

Hello. I'm Max's mom. I want to thank you for purchasing his book and sharing it with others. In 2014, my 12-year-old son Max came up with the idea of sharing his story to help other kids on the autism spectrum.

This book is the result of an art show that Max put together. Max's display was entitled "Insight into the Autistic Mind." His drawings and essays were displayed, primarily to educate people on how different his experience is compared to kids who are "neurotypical." His art show was very well-received, and he wanted to take his message to a larger audience. The result is his book, **Hello, MY Name is Max, and I Have Autism**.

Many have asked if I helped him write the book. Honestly, my role has been as a scribe, financial aid, transportation, and press secretary. The words and the images belong to Max.

The art show was conceived by Max approaching me for permission to do a service project to benefit the food bank that helped us during a time of need. I agreed, but he needed an umbrella to work under to pitch his food drive. It occurred to us that World Autism Day was on April 2nd. Max took this idea and concocted a plan with another ASD kid to have a school-wide celebration about autism awareness that would include a canned food drive.

As a result, Eagleview Elementary hosted its first-ever "Light it up BLUE" Autism Awareness Day. Max and his friend read fact sheets to classrooms about autism and opened themselves up for a question and answer session.

The students and staff all dressed in blue on the day and participated in signing a Pledge of Compassion, adding it to the school's Compassion Wall. Max's art and essays hung in the main hall, and the kids collected a fantastic amount of food for the local pantry. I was excited to see the school get behind these kids and let them celebrate "neurodiversity."

The celebration was extra special as Eagleview was the first elementary school in the county to offer instruction to ASD students. Max was one of six students chosen to pilot the program. The program was so successful that five other ASD programs opened. In a way, Max's event was a way of saying, "thank you" as it brought positive media attention to the program and the need to sustain special education funding. It also highlighted the success of the Eagleview Model. The school plans to do the event every year, and Max has been invited back to speak at a student assembly.

In all fairness, my son did have some help with his project. The construction of the art show was a family affair. I helped with the cutting and pasting of the work as well as many trips to Michaels. I would sit with my laptop as he dictated to me what he wanted to say in his essays. I would type, then I would read back what he told me, and he would make changes. I hung the art in the hall with the help of his art teacher.

It was a special moment for me to see Max's art and essays displayed because I knew it was powerful, and it took a lot of guts to do it. The response to his show was truly unexpected. His words and images touched so many people, adults and children alike.

The greatest gift was my participation in helping write Max's essays. It was an overwhelming experience to hear him describe life on the spectrum. I learned more about autism in two weeks than I did in the past 12 years. Some of the essays were hard for me to type as I was close to tears. His wisdom and insight moved me. I also felt embarrassed by my ignorance of my son's needs and admonished myself for my impatience with him. The experience made us closer as we are both learning how to negotiate life on the spectrum.

I say this many times—he is the guru, the teacher. I may be his mother, but I am learning more about life and God from my 12-year-old son than I did in my years at University. I am honored to be a part of this process and to be chosen as his mother.

We hope to have this book be used as a tool to create compassion, awareness, and understanding for kids on the spectrum. Autism appears in many expressions. Some severe, some in patterns, some come and go. It's not always obvious. It's easy to get frustrated, and it's normal to want to give up. Tears are frequent, as is anger, but the child is still there. That light is still there. Even those who cannot speak may appear to be so separate from us. They know love. Kids on the spectrum need those who are not to be patient, compassionate, and educate themselves about autism.

Max said that he wants to be a voice for the kids who cannot speak. He has a unique perspective. My son was non-verbal and in his own world for a long time. It was so severe that I was advised to surrender him to the State and have Max institutionalized. He was deemed "unteachable," and that he would never thrive.

Never go to school, dress himself, feed himself—that he was hopeless. I remember sitting there hearing these words and looking at my son. I saw how the light danced in his eyes, and I rejected the "expert's" diagnoses. I pushed forward and kept trying to reach him. Max and I were impoverished and had limited resources, so I made up things as we went along. Bouncing on the bed and repeating letters, massage, Reiki, essential oils, diet, exercise, music—we tried everything. It was painful for both of us. Then, one day, he started talking. By age 10, he read for the first time and could tie his shoes. By 12, he was at grade level, skateboarding, playing PS3, and loves Sherlock Holmes. It was a miracle.

Experience begets compassion. Max remembers what that was like, not being able to speak. He remembers his struggles in trying to communicate with me and how he would get angry or cry. Therefore, Max is very gentle with the kids who are non-verbal. Max is highly intuitive, and he told me that he knows what the non-verbal kids are trying to say. I've watched my son interact with these little ones, and he stops, listens, and shakes his head, and talks to them. It's like they have a way of communication of their own. I cannot explain this intellectually. He seems to connect in a way that, as an adult, I cannot understand. So, it is literal when he says he wants to speak for the kids who cannot. That is one thing about kids with autism—they are VERY literal.

It was a hard road for Max to get to where he is today. He suffered an amazing amount of discrimination and exclusion because of his disability. Instead of being bitter, he's now an advocate for himself and others on the spectrum. The other day he told me that "we were all just walking each other home." No need for anger, just love.

It is our sincere hope that you enjoy his book and that you take something away from it. It was written in love with the intention of creating understanding and making space for kids like Max. A space to express as they can express; to sing, dance, repeat and stim and flap, and smile, to do so in a place of honor and light and love. To just be...

Max's mom.

INTRODUCTION

My name is Max, and I have autism. This label just means that I'm different, not damaged. My mom tells me this all the time. She says my brain is just wired differently.

I didn't know I had autism until last year. I knew I had "it," but I didn't really understand it. My mom didn't want me to be held back by a label. When I realized what it was, I got really depressed and hated myself. I hated my autism as I knew it made people feel uncomfortable around me. My mom heard me talking to myself about how I wished the autism in me would die. She started crying and told me that it was the autism that made me who I am, and she was really sad that I hated a part of myself.

My Uncle Dean gave me an art set, and my mom told me that the best way for me to deal with my autism was to embrace it. She said that yes, I was different but to focus on my strengths, not what others perceived as my weakness. She encouraged me to draw my feelings, to get them out on paper. It made me feel better.

Our family believes that it is our duty to help others. My artwork and my book is how I am paying it forward. It was hard trying to negotiate being an autistic kid in a neurotypical world. I was kicked out of schools, YMCA basketball, Cub Scouts, even McDonalds. People didn't understand that I was different as my disability wasn't obvious. It's not like we turn purple or something. I wish people could have been more patient with me and my mom. It would have made a huge difference.

My art show is entitled, Insight into the Autistic Mind. I took my show and made it into this book. I'm sharing it because I want to generate compassion for other kids, just like me. Especially the ones who cannot speak. They need someone to speak for them. Someone who is just like them, not someone who read a book or wrote a thesis in college. Someone who knows what it is like to be overwhelmed, or not being able to talk or misunderstood.

Someone like me.

My name is Max. And I have autism. Autism, yep... it's just part of who I am!

CHAPTER ONE

<u>WHAT DOES AUTISM LOOK LIKE?</u>

Self-portrait

I did this picture at school. It became part of a larger work entitled, "My Family," which was part of the Community Quilt at the Denver Art Museum. My mom had to submit an artist bio for me. She asked me what my art was about. This is what she wrote and what was published in a book about the Community Quilt.

My son's piece is entitled "My Family." Max used cutouts from family photos to recreate the self-portrait that he did in art class. There is a photo of the self-portrait in the upper left, and in the bottom right, a picture of Max.

Max is a high-functioning autistic and was non-verbal until the age of 6. He has been subject to segregation and prejudice since he was quite young. Max was denied educational and social opportunities due to his diagnosis. After several rejections, we finally found an autism program. The interventions worked. Max is now in a regular classroom with his peers but still feels separate. He is aware of his autism but considers it a label versus a definition.

His art reflects his view of his identity. He is able to be his own person and defy his labeling. He is not just autistic. He is an 11-year-old boy, a blend of his entire family and his life experiences. Max placed pictures of his family around his self-portrait. He knows his family surrounds him and protects him, but he can still be his own person.

Max said, "I am not autistic. I am ME."

I knew I had autism, but it is like being labeled a Lutheran or a Toyota. I didn't know exactly what it was about until later. I am glad I had my family to surround me when I did finally figure it out.

So what does autism look like? Like ME!

CHAPTER TWO

<u>HOW DID YOU GET AUTISM?</u>

Needles I Hate

When I go to the doctor, I really don't like getting shots. It's hard for me as I don't want a chemical in my body forced inside of me. I wish I could drink it, but that's not what the rules say. It's not fair as my mom got the polio vaccine on a sugar cube. I wish I could drink it because I don't want a sharp thing in my arm, even though I have to take it and I don't like it. It hurts. It really hurts.

There is a theory that my autism was caused by my getting these shots. That's not true. God made me autistic. The shots didn't make me autistic. God sat there and asked the angels who should have autism, and they chose me. The angels said I should have autism so I can make a difference in this world.

I am doing this through my drawing and writing. I want to explain how autistic kids might feel in ordinary situations. You can't see in my head. I'm lucky because I can talk, but the words get stuck. Drawing helps me get the words out.

I want to be a voice for every single child who has autism and who cannot speak. The kids who can't speak are just like me. We are not like everyone else. We can't see other people's feelings or do well in school or pay attention. Just because we can't be like everyone else doesn't mean we don't matter. We do matter.

All we need is a little compassion.

CHAPTER THREE

<u>DOES AUTISM GO AWAY?</u>

I'm Stuck With It.

The autism is stuck in my hand. I'm making a fist, trying to keep it in my hand. The red is my rage about how I wanted to keep the autism in my hand and stop it from moving through my body. The autism is the blue that is trying to escape. The yellow is the power of me trying to keep the autism in my hand. The battle between the autism and the rage is what made my hand and arm bleed. The black vessels in the red kept moving the autism down into my body and the war kept raging. The autism cannot shrink. It will not go away. It's stuck in there. The rage tried to make it get smaller and smaller and then poof! It would go away. No matter how much the rage tries its very best, the autism is stuck, so I guess I'm just stuck with it.

When I learned about how I have autism, I cried while I was in the shower. I wished the autism would die. My mom heard me and she handed me the art set that my Uncle Dean gave me for my birthday. She told me to draw about what it is like to have autism. The drawing helped me feel better. My mom loves me as I am. I guess that is good because the autism isn't going anywhere.

Sometimes I wish I was normal, but I was picked by the angels. I remember the angels. When I was born, I looked up and I thought I saw one but it was my mom. I remember thinking, OH, that's my mom because she didn't have any wings and she didn't glow.

CHAPTER FOUR

<u>WHAT IS IT LIKE FOR YOU IN THE CLASSROOM?</u>

The Classroom

The classroom is really hard for someone like me. This is a drawing of how I feel every day in my classroom.

Red waves are coming after me while I sit at my desk. This represents how I interact with other people and distractions. One of the waves might be a classmate going against me or saying something mean to me. Another wave is the assignment, but kids are distracting me, and I miss the instructions.

My anger bubbles up. This is the blue—my frustration with the drama in my classroom. I have to read and write and listen all at the same time.

The black is my brain core. It's really dark. When I am in a good mood, it's white and green, but when I get upset, it turns black.

I feel upset sometimes in the classroom. My stomach hurts, and I want to go home. I feel overwhelmed and small. I just want to shrink down and vanish.

I sit by myself because I don't want to be near anyone. My friends might think I'm claustrophobic, but I'm just irritated when I have to be around others, especially when I have to concentrate.

I really hate it when I have to pick a partner. I like to sit by myself. I have to walk around to find someone, but usually the kids pick their friends, and I'm left out anyways. I end up staying by myself, and that is just fine by me. I sort of wish I had a buddy, but I'm ok on my own.

I appreciate people wanting me to join their table or be my buddy. I'll do it, but I'm happiest when I can sit by myself. That way I can calm down and actually learn something. So if you see me sitting by myself, I'm not lonely. I'm ok. If I want to be with you, I'll initiate it. No offense.

CHAPTER FIVE

<u>HOW COME YOU GET UPSET SO EASILY?</u>

Frustration

Sometimes I feel frustrated when I get an assignment, but I have no idea what it is about.

Since I have autism, I get pulled out of my class for tutoring and therapies. As a result, I miss the instruction. So I get my assignments when I get back and have no clue what to do.

Then, when I am in class, I am trying really hard to listen and remember what my teacher said. I have to repeat the instructions over and over in my head. If someone nearby is talking for more than three minutes, I can't think. It drives me crazy, and I get really frustrated.

I hate getting frustrated because it feels like I am hurting someone's feelings. I don't want to hurt anyone. That is never my wish.

Sometimes I just need to walk away.

CHAPTER SIX

<u>HOW COME YOU LEAVE CLASS ALL THE TIME?</u>

I Need A Break

When I am working in the classroom or even just hanging out with my family or friends, sometimes I need a break. The traffic around me gets to be too much. It feels like my brain is filling up with garbage. I get a headache, and I need to walk away, just to empty out the garbage that is filling up my mind.

My brain is symbolized in my drawing by the following: the buildings on the sides and the front is my brain. The bridge provides a way for the people and the cars to cross. It connects one side of my brain to the other side.

When the traffic gets too congested or there are too many people, they fall into the valley of garbage. The traffic appears when I have to think too much or have too many thoughts all at once.

When there are too many people, even in real life, they can't stay on the path. They start pushing each other and go into the street. The cars crash and the people fall off the bridge. This is how I feel when there are too many people doing too many things all at once. Someone will get hurt. Usually, that person is me.

So please be patient with me while I take out the trash.

CHAPTER SEVEN

WHY DO YOU TAKE THINGS SO LITERALLY? CAN'T YOU TELL THAT I'M KIDDING?

Acceptance of Myself.

First, this is a real thing that just happened last week. I felt pretty terrible after skateboarding. I felt like everyone was looking at me, and everyone is watching me, and they think I suck, even though I practice really hard. They look at me weird and I feel like I don't belong there. So I went outside and just sat there, talking to myself and my skateboard. I leaned on the brick wall, just looking at my board and watching people outside. My mom dropped me off, so I had to deal with this on my own.

The purple on the page means the skills. The red is how I am angry at my lack of skills, and the blue is my frustration at how other people look at me when I skate. My friend Andrew gives me a hard time at school about how I can't skate and how I got my board from Walmart, which isn't true. My mom saved her money and bought me a very expensive board from World Industries as she wants me to skate and get exercise.

I am pretty good at sports, but I get frustrated. It takes me longer to learn something new. But I really like going to Progresh. I have been landing my ollies and doing better. I have learned to accept the fact that I have to practice longer than other kids. I also realized that the kids probably were not judging me and that Andrew is teasing me because that's what best friends do. This is part of my autism—I misinterpret things, and I take things literally. I am trying to understand the concept of irony and symbolism. It's a quirky trait of mine. I have accepted it.

CHAPTER EIGHT

<u>WHAT MAKES YOU HAPPY...CAN YOU FEEL HAPPY?</u>

Happy Land

This is a picture that shows that I am happy. Some things make me happier than others. First, I like it when I'm not in school. Like Winter Break or Spring Break. I can stay home and play video games or draw or go to Progresh.

The person in the middle is me, drinking root beer. Root beer makes me happy. There are cats in the drawing because I love all of my cats. Bob, Fuzzy, Felix and Oscar. I care for every single animal except for big dogs that bite me. I don't like that.

Video games makes me happy, especially Little Big Planet. I also like to watch TV but I can't tell you the show as it is a BIG SECRET between me and my mom. Oh, and my other Brony friends. So I guess the secret is not that big.

You see, kids with autism can feel joy. We can also love. We are not always frustrated or angry or not feeling anything. We are just as joyful as the next person. We just have different ways of showing it.

Sometimes our happiness can appear as obsessive and when our things that make us happy disappear, like when I broke my controller on my PS3, boy, was I upset. Luckily, my grandmother gave my mom a gift card for Christmas and my mom replaced it. Whew!

When you have autism, you collect things or hoard things. You have a notebook and write things down. It is very important to me to have my Magic Cards in their separate piles. When I was little, I needed my cars lined up and my dog, Buggie, so I could sleep. I need order in my disordered world.

It may seem weird to you, but it makes me happy.

CHAPTER NINE

<u>THERE ARE SO MANY THINGS THAT MAKE US DIFFERENT.</u>
<u>WHAT MAKES US THE SAME?</u>

Thirsty for Happiness

Do you know how you feel when you eat or drink something or do something to make yourself feel better? I'm just like that myself. There's a drink that is called root beer. I like drinking this drink as it makes me feel better. I like the taste, the texture, and the core of a root beer float. You can use this drink many ways—root beer float, drink it, put ice in it. The best way is in a frosty mug! I prefer this drink as it makes me feel better and it's delicious. I know I'm not the only person who likes drinks like these.

See, we aren't so different after all!

IN CONCLUSION

I realized that autism is just part of who I am. It is me, but it doesn't define me. I just need some help in life. I'm lucky. My family has my back. My mom is my biggest support. She's the one who got me into a school that didn't kick me out. She pushes me academically. (Sometimes, just a little bit TOO hard as she forgets about my autism.) So I'm lucky. I have my mom who wants me to do well in school and go to college. My mom also encourages my art and music. My grandparents have always believed in me, and I have friends, teachers, and lots of aunts and uncles who cheer me on. My mom is the best. She didn't give up on me, even when she was told by doctors that there wasn't any hope.

My mom said that she saw light in my eyes. She knew I was there. I know what she is talking about. I see it too, in the other kids. By that, I mean the kids like me. It's hard. I know, to be around kids like me. But please, give us a chance. Don't give up! And to kids like me, just be yourself. That is what makes YOU!!!

You are AWESOME. We are awesome!

Your friend,

Max

ACKNOWLEDGEMENTS

I would like to acknowledge the people who made this book possible.

A special thanks to the following people who contributed money and time to make this book a reality for Max.

Cynthia Glasson, Joe Bonadonna, Sally Tibbetts, Nina Morningstar, Mary Lou Iverson, Lloyd Barger, Dianne Winkler, Sue Ernest.

Thank you to all my Facebook friends for sharing our fundraising posts and for all the words of encouragement when things were looking down. Thank you to Autism Speaks, Autism Society and Firefly for inviting Max to display his art and talk about his message.

And a thank you for helping Max become the young man he is today.

Eagleview Elementary faculty and staff: Scott Dowen, Frank Saporano, Damon Graham-Haradon, Lea Mitchel, Julie Sapena, Popi Hute, Keri Odekirk, Laura Rigel, Dani Bondurant, Julie Vigil, and the very first teacher, affectionately known as Miss Kim.

Of course, thanks to Uncle Dean Williams, who gave Max the art set that put all of this in motion.

From Max's Mom: A note to newly diagnosed families.

You have joined a unique club. The initiation was long, and now you know the secret of our society. We are the parents of autistic children, and what do we do?

We worry.

And we react, we advocate, we explain, we apologize, we arrange, we rearrange, we have plans, and then two or three backup plans. We are the moms and dads with the extra bag of clothes in the car. We know where to find the missing toy because the world will truly end if we don't. We cringe when the car playing loud bass pulls up next to us. We bite our lip when a stranger asks us what's wrong with our kids, of how they just need a spanking, or how we can't control our child. We stop breathing for a moment when we drop our child off at school, checking our phone, waiting for the call to pick them up immediately. We try to hold a job. We may even try to go back to school. Every day is a maneuver, an adjustment, a challenge. We lock ourselves in the bathroom and cry, maybe with a bottle of cheap red wine with a screw-off cap, sitting at our feet while our Facebook friends send us stickers and pokes, attempting to cheer us up. We feel pangs of jealousy when we hear about other kids' accomplishments. We feel resentful and sad and get angry at God.

It's normal.

We also find such joy in the small things. Every goal reached is cause for celebration. Seeing our child light up with a smile makes us melt. When our little ones are finally asleep, we can admire their grace. They made it through an entire day at school. They slept five hours. They learned how to dress, put socks on, keep socks on. Every moment is precious. Every movement, breath, smile, accomplishment is worth every moment of worry.

Don't worry so much.

My advice to you, newly diagnosed parents, is to focus on what your child can do. There is a saying in our club—if you met one person with autism, you met one person with autism. Every child with autism is different. Celebrate and nourish what they can do and help it grow.

Be a b****

Advocate for yourself and your child. You know what works for them. Don't be afraid to speak your mind. Ask for services. Ask for IEP reviews. Be aware of your rights, and don't be scared to fight for them.

Be grateful

Every day is a gift—even the bad ones. Be grateful for what you have but don't be afraid to ask for more.

Get connected

Find autism support groups and talk to them. There are so many sources of funding and information that can help you and your child. It's exhausting being a mom on the spectrum. If a friend asks how they can help, hand them the laptop and get them to do some research for you.

Be kind to yourself

This was not your fault. Don't listen to the people who suggest that it was. We don't know what causes autism. There is no point in blaming yourself, the father for old sperm or the mother for being "a refrigerator", the environment, the vaccines, the food supply, the electrical wires...it's easy to get sucked into this blame game. What matters most is what you do now.

Read all about it

But question what you read. Even my words you should question. I'm not an expert. I'm just a mom. My experience may not match yours. Pick your sources and go from there. Pub Med, Mayo Clinic, NIH, John Hopkins—lots to choose from. Check your local ASD groups for referrals. The larger clearinghouses are an excellent place to start.

Allow Yourself to grieve.

We all enter this parenthood game with ideas of how it should be. Then, it doesn't quite turn out the way that we think it should. Add the fact that there is this weird competition between moms and the ongoing fight between stay-at-home moms and working moms…UGH. The mommy wars are brutal. If you are a single dad, you find yourself outnumbered as the majority of single parents ASD families are women led. Regardless, when your kid is special needs, it changes the game. We get left out. Our friends and family may disappear. We don't get to go to Disneyland. We don't get invited to birthday parties. A day at the waterpark, a parade, even McDonald's play place—not for us. It's a loss. Go ahead and cry. Getting the diagnosis IS a loss. A loss of an idealized future. A loss of "normal." It's ok to feel the loss. Get it out. Write about it. Just don't bottle it up, as it will come back to hurt you later.

Don't fight the current, as it is going to drag you along anyways.

One of my mistakes early on was trying to force my son into my life. I wanted to go to nursing school. I wanted to have a "real" job. I wanted to have an everyday life, but after losing countless jobs, 30 plus babysitters, having to drop out of school eight times, I finally made the wise choice of not fighting the current. Instead, I became a massage therapist and worked around my son. Sure, I was dirt poor. I AM dirt poor, but I was available for my son. If you have a partner, divide the tasks up into who does what best, not by gender or "it's your turn" or "it's your job." Save that for changing the cat box.

Be Here Now.

Be in the present. Our little ones grow up so fast. Enjoy what you have right now as each day, each year presents something new.

Be Love Now.

Love your child. Love yourself.

Welcome to Alpha Sigma Delta, ASD FAM! There are so many of us ASD parents out there. Just reach out and connect with a group. You are not alone in this. Our community sticks together and helps each other out.

You are not alone.

Epilogue

August 2021

Max and I had an opportunity to provide a revision to his book, and it is with great excitement that I can update what has transpired since 2014.

Multiple school districts picked up his book and colleges, libraries, and families, and yes, he did reach his goal of providing comfort and education for young people on the autism spectrum. His book is known all over the world.

Max launched his non-profit Blue Ribbon Arts Initiative and has held art shows featuring young people with autism since 2014. We've given away at least 100 art start kits to young people who needed them, negotiated sensory-friendly mornings at the Denver Art Museum as well as sensory-friendly concerts with the Colorado Symphony. We provided art for the NEST sensory time-out at the Children's Museum, held a show in Chicago, participated as headliners in This Spectrum Life at the University of Northern Iowa, spoke at numerous conferences--we've been BUSY advocating for and connecting our spectrum friends to the arts.

And during this time, Max kept working hard at his personal development, education, and playing the saxophone. In middle school, Max's music teacher, Mr. David Wiske, made the bold choice to include a kid on the spectrum in his band room. Max's life changed. He fell in love with playing the saxophone. A friend of mine from middle school days, Jennifer Frazzini, gave him the instrument. Another friend, Donald Rossa, allowed us to sneak in the back at his jazz club during Friday Lunch Club, and Max fell in love with Jazz.

Learning music opened up another neural pathway for Max. It allowed him to learn math. This allowed him to be released from SLS classes at Rocky Top. He excelled at band and became more confident. Soon, Max was in high school and eventually made the top bands at Horizon High under the direction of Tim Dailey. Max was bold and insisted on having his IEP reduced to the minimum. It was hard, but he pressed on, and in 2021, Max graduated from Horizon High in the middle of the pandemic. Max was accepted into every college he applied to and was interviewed by Harvard. While Max didn't get into Harvard, he did get accepted into the School of Music at the University of Northern Colorado. He received a large scholarship from the Masonic Grand Lodge for his community service work which enabled him to attend.

Max is majoring in Music Education K-12 and Jazz performance with a certificate in special education. He wants to be a band teacher when he graduates and provide the same inclusion that Mr. Wiske did for him for any kid who wants to play. When asked why, Max said, "It's my way of paying it forward." I'm so proud of him.

In the quiet of my home, I reflected on how our lives are so different now. When I did this edit, I eliminated some credits. In 2015, we finally broke away from some very toxic people in our lives and found that we did much better when they were gone. I became a nurse and lifted us out of poverty. I met a wonderful man who, in turn, has two spectrumites himself. We blended our families, and our lives are now peaceful, abundant, and filled with love versus anger and narcissism.

Our work with Blue Ribbon Arts Initiative continues, but without Max at the helm. UNC requires his full attention. I miss him. I'm in awe of how far he has come. The boy deemed "unteachable" and "unreachable" grew to become the man playing in a Big Band ensemble in college. All because we chose not to give up, and we were blessed with people who didn't give up on us.

Max thrived.